I0841750

Dad family chart

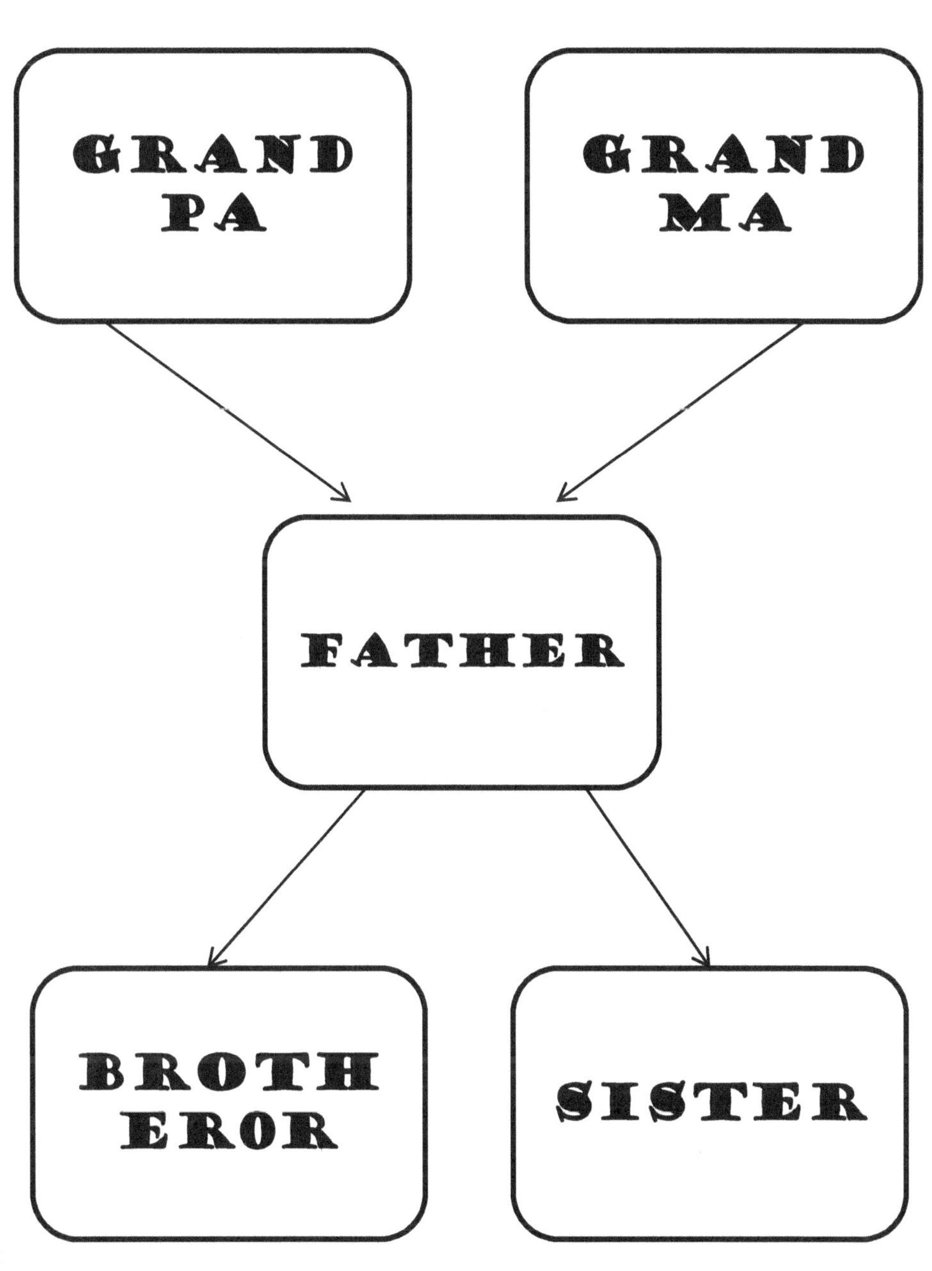

1: When I was litlle, what did you think I was going to be when I grew up?

2. Do you think I have more of your good qualities or bad qualities?

3. What is the funniest thing I ever said or did as a kid?

4 WHEN WAS THE FIRST TIME YOU HEARD ME CURSE?

5 describe How much you love me dad?

6. What would you have named me if I was the opposite gender?

7 How did my mom get married?

8. Which children's book did you read to me the most when I was little?

9. What was the most annoying thing I did as a baby?

10 what is the thing i dreamed of doing ?

11. How did you choose my middle name?

12. Which one of my school friends did you hate having over?

13. Whatwere my very first words?

14. What's your all-time favorite picture of me?

15. Did you want me to be a boy or a girl?

16 Do you think i will succeed and why ?

17. What is your very first memory of me?

18. What's the first toy you ever remember buying me?

19. Did you find out my gender before I was born or after?

20 do you want to raise anther family ?

21. Did you ever drop me as a baby?

22. When you were my age, did you want kids?

23. What made me cry the most when I was little?

24. What made me laugh the most when I was little?

25. What TV show would I watch every single day?

26. Did you ever lose me in the supermarket or anywhere else?

27. What was the first movie you brought me to the theater to see?

28. What song did I listen to on repeat when I was super young?

29. What was the nicest thing I ever said to you?

30. What was the meanest thing I ever said to you?

31. What was my favorite stuffed animal?

32. What age (of mine) did you hate experiencing the most?

33. What age (of mine) do you feel like we were closest?

34. What's the first word that comes to mind when you hear my name?

35 .What do you regret?

36. Which one of the parents at my school annoyed you the most?

37 What is the worst part about being my father?

38. What is the best part about being my father?

39. What was my favorite flavor of baby food?

40 What is my worst habit

41. Which television character reminds you of me the most?

42. What song reminds you of me the most?

43. What family member did you try to keep far away from me

44. Did I ever do anything creepy as a kid that scared you?

45. Was I a faster or slower learner than everyone else in class?

46. What was the best drawing I ever made for you?

47. What was I the most afraid of as a child?

48. Is there anything about our family history you've kept a secret?

49. Overall, did you consider me a good kid?

50. Are you happy with the way I turned out?